CLT

EXAM STUDY GUIDE

2024-2025

- ▮ **Crafting an Effective Study Plan:** Uncover the secrets to developing a customized study strategy tailored to your needs, optimizing productivity while minimizing time wastage.
- 💬 **Unlocking Cognitive Potential:** Discover proven methods for enhancing memory retention, boosting comprehension levels, and cementing information in your long-term memory.
- ⏰ **Balancing Act:** Utilize effective time management techniques to strike a harmonious balance between your study commitments and other obligations, fostering a healthy work-life-study equilibrium.
- 🏆 **Stress Management Solutions:** Conquer exam-related stress through mindfulness practices, relaxation techniques, and resilience-building exercises, ensuring a calm and focused mindset during crucial moments.
- ▮ **The Power of Practice:** Delve into the significance of practice exams, sample questions, and simulated tests, and uncover strategies for analyzing performance to pinpoint areas ripe for improvement.

Disclaimer of Liability:

TABLE OF CONTENT

Introduction

Welcome to "The Complete CLT Exam Study Guide" for the 2024-2025 season. This comprehensive guide is designed to assist students in preparing for the Classic Learning Test (CLT), a rigorous examination that evaluates critical thinking, logic, and reasoning skills. Whether you're a first-time test taker or aiming to improve your score, this book will provide you with the necessary tools and strategies to excel on the CLT.

Chapter 1: Understanding the CLT

What is the CLT?
Purpose and significance of the CLT
Structure and format of the CLT
Scoring and score interpretation

Chapter 2: CLT Sections Breakdown

Verbal Reasoning
Types of questions
Strategies for comprehension and analysis
Vocabulary building techniques
Grammar/Writing
Grammar rules and concepts tested
Essay writing strategies
Practice prompts and sample essays
Quantitative Reasoning
Math concepts covered
Problem-solving techniques
Tips for managing time
Ethics & Logic
Topics covered
Logical reasoning strategies
Ethical reasoning and dilemma-solving

Chapter 3: Preparation Strategies

Setting realistic goals
Creating a study schedule
Utilizing practice tests and resources
Tips for effective studying
Managing test anxiety

Chapter 4: Practice Questions and Exams

Verbal Reasoning practice questions
Grammar/Writing practice exercises
Quantitative Reasoning practice problems
Ethics & Logic scenarios
Full-length practice exams

Chapter 5: Additional Resources

Recommended books and study materials
Online resources and practice websites
Tutoring services and study groups
CLT official resources

Chapter 6: Test Day Tips

Preparing for test day
What to expect on exam day
Strategies for each section
Managing time during the exam
After the test: next steps

Chapter 7: Advanced Techniques for Each Section

Verbal Reasoning: Advanced comprehension strategies, deep analysis techniques, critical reading exercises.
Grammar/Writing: Advanced grammar concepts, advanced essay writing tips, rhetorical analysis exercises.

Quantitative Reasoning: Advanced problem-solving strategies, complex math concepts, advanced quantitative reasoning drills.
Ethics & Logic: Advanced logical reasoning techniques, advanced ethical reasoning scenarios, practice with complex logical puzzles.

Chapter 8: Targeted Skill Improvement

Identifying weaknesses and strengths
Tailoring study plans to address specific areas of improvement
Targeted practice exercises for each section
Tracking progress and adjusting study strategies accordingly

Overview

Using our in-depth study guide, you may begin your journey to mastering the Classic Learning Test (CLT) for the 2024–2025 exam cycle. More than just an entrance exam, the CLT serves as a key to chances for further study and personal development. This guide is an essential tool for anyone navigating the complexities of the CLT, be they a high school student hoping to get into a top university or a lifelong learner looking to push themselves.

The CLT's Significance

Standardized examinations are a crucial component of assessing students' ability and potential in the competitive academic environment of today. Amid the sea of standardized exams, the CLT stands out as a beacon of intellectual engagement with its emphasis on reasoning, ethical discernment, and critical thinking. The purpose of the CLT is to evaluate a candidate's depth of understanding and practical application of knowledge, in contrast to other standardized examinations that place a strong emphasis on memorization and repetition of facts.

The CLT's evolution

From the beginning, educators, colleges, and students have all praised and acknowledged the CLT. The CLT was created as a substitute for conventional college entrance tests, but it has since developed into a dynamic assessment instrument that encourages ethical reasoning and intellectual curiosity in addition to measuring academic aptitude. The CLT is continuously improving its structure and content with each iteration to guarantee that it is applicable and efficient in assessing students' preparedness for postsecondary education.

A Comprehensive Method for Preparation

It takes more than just studying arithmetic problems and memorizing vocabulary lists to be ready for the CLT. It necessitates a comprehensive strategy that includes ethical reasoning, critical thinking abilities, and test-taking techniques. This study guide has been painstakingly created to give you the whole toolkit you need to ace the CLT. We can help you every step of the way, from comprehending the sophisticated concepts and strategies to mastering the exam's structure and format.

How to Use the Guide

This manual is broken up into multiple chapters, each of which focuses on a different facet of being ready for CLT. The ensuing chapters comprise the following:

Chapter 1: Understanding the CLT provides a thorough explanation of the CLT's goals, composition, and scoring system.
Chapter 2: Analysis of CLT Sections: comprehensive breakdown of every CLT segment, including approaches and pointers for overcoming it.
Chapter 3: Study Strategies: Tried-and-true methods for organizing your studies, managing your time, and getting over exam anxiety.
Chapter 4: Sample Test Questions and Answers a wealth of practice resources to support your study, such as full-length practice tests, activities, and example questions.
Chapter 5: Supplementary Resources: Tips for Better Preparation: More reading materials, internet sites, and tutoring services.
Chapter 6: Test Day Tips: Useful guidance for organizing your schedule, maximizing your performance, and navigating test day.
In summary

As you begin your CLT preparation process, keep in mind that success is more than just getting a good score; it's also about developing a lifelong learning, critical thinking, and ethical discernment mentality. You can conquer the CLT and walk out with pride if you put in the effort, stay with it, and follow the advice in our study guide. Together, let's go out on this adventure and open the doors to a world of intellectual and academic fulfillment.

Chapter 1: Getting to Know the CLT

We explore in detail the fundamental components of the Classic Learning Test (CLT) in this chapter. For efficient preparation, it is essential to comprehend the CLT from its inception to its structure and importance.

History and Objectives

The Classic Learning Test, or CLT for short, was created in reaction to what people felt were flaws in more established standardized assessments like the SAT and ACT. The CLT was developed as an alternative evaluation by Jeremy Tate in 2015. It was intended to give more weight to logical reasoning, ethical judgment, and critical thinking than to rote memorization and formulaic problem-solving.

In contrast to its competitors, the CLT is influenced by the classical education paradigm, which places a strong emphasis on developing morality, wisdom, and a love of study. The CLT seeks to give colleges and universities a more comprehensive assessment of students' preparedness for higher education by moving the emphasis from restricted subject-specific knowledge to wider intellectual talents.

Form and Organization

Verbal Reasoning, Grammar/Writing, Quantitative Reasoning, and Ethics & Logic are the four components that make up the CLT. The purpose of each segment is to evaluate particular cognitive skills and moral precepts that are critical for success in college and beyond.

Verbal Reasoning: This portion assesses students' comprehension, analysis, and ability to recognize important concepts in written passages and make logical deductions. The questions can include anything from textual analysis and critical reasoning to reading comprehension.

Grammar/Writing: Students' understanding of English grammar, syntax, and usage is assessed in this part. Students must also produce an essay in response to a prompt, showcasing their capacity for persuasive and cogent idea expression.

Quantitative Reasoning: Students' mathematical knowledge, problem-solving techniques, and quantitative reasoning skills are evaluated in this area. Numerous math areas, such as algebra, geometry, and data interpretation, may be covered in the questions.

Ethics & Logic: This special segment assesses students' capacity for both logical and ethical reasoning. Pupils are asked to evaluate arguments, spot fallacies, and form morally sound conclusions in response to moral conundrums and logical riddles.

Because the CLT is administered digitally, more accessibility and flexibility are possible. Examiners can select from a number of test dates offered throughout the year and take the examination in the convenience of their own homes or at approved testing locations.

Evaluation and Explanation

Unlike conventional standardized examinations, the CLT scoring system uses a comprehensive methodology that considers both the quantitative and qualitative components of performance. A maximum total score of 480 is possible, with scores ranging from 0 to 120 for each segment.

Students receive a percentile ranking that shows how they performed in relation to other test-takers in addition to their numerical scores. This percentile score aids in the decision-making process for admissions at colleges and universities by offering insightful information about a student's position within the applicant pool.

It's crucial to remember that the CLT gives topic mastery and critical thinking abilities equal weight. A strong grasp of academic concepts is necessary to get good grades, but so is the capacity for critical thought, information analysis, and knowledge application in new situations.

Importance and Advantages

Higher education's objectives are strongly aligned with the CLT's emphasis on critical thinking, ethical reasoning, and intellectual engagement. The CLT aims to identify students who are not only academically successful but also intellectually curious, morally upright, and capable of making significant contributions to society by giving these qualities precedence above basic content knowledge.

The CLT provides higher education institutions with a more detailed and nuanced assessment of candidates' chances of success. Institutions can more accurately determine whether candidates are prepared for the demands of higher education and beyond by taking into account not only what they know but also how they reason and think.

Furthermore, the CLT's dedication to diversity and accessibility guarantees that students from a variety of backgrounds can demonstrate their skills and pursue their academic goals. With various test dates, digital administration, and cost waivers available to qualified students, the CLT aims to provide equal opportunities and enable every student to pursue their aspirations of a college degree.

In conclusion, the CLT is a paradigm change in standardized testing that puts an emphasis on holistic learning, ethical judgment, and intellectual engagement. Students can take the test with confidence and start their journey toward both academic and personal progress if they grasp the history, format, scoring, and importance of the CLT.

Chapter 2: Breakdown of CLT Sections

We will examine a thorough dissection of every component of the Classic Learning Test (CLT) in this chapter. To succeed in the test, one must comprehend the subtleties of each section and know how to approach them effectively.

Oral Reasoning

The purpose of the CLT's Verbal Reasoning portion is to evaluate students' comprehension of written passages, analysis of arguments, and ability to make logical deductions. Multiple-choice questions testing several facets of reading comprehension and critical thinking abilities make up this part.

Questions Types:

Reading Comprehension: Students' capacity to comprehend and analyze textual passages is evaluated by these questions. Examinees may be required to list the key concepts, describe the author's position or argument, and deduce word or phrase meanings from context.

Critical Reasoning: In critical reasoning tasks, students are presented with claims or arguments and asked to assess their persuasiveness, recognize presumptions, spot logical fallacies, and come to a sound conclusion.

Textual Analysis: Textual analysis questions concentrate on examining a passage's tone, structure, and rhetorical devices. Pupils could be asked to name literary devices, understand the author's intention or goal, and assess how well the paragraph communicates its point.

Success Techniques:

Active Reading: As you read, actively participate in the passage by stressing key points, making important annotations, and summarizing the essential ideas.

Determine Important Elements: Keep an eye out for the author's argument or point of view as well as the main concept and any supporting information. To determine the author's tone, goal, and target audience, look for hints.

Examine Arguments: Develop your ability to recognize the logical connections, premises, and conclusions in arguments. Keep an eye out for supporting details, presumptions, and possible logic errors.

Practice Frequently: Learn how to read and respond to a variety of passage formats and question kinds. Your critical thinking and reading comprehension skills will both benefit from this.

Organize Your Time Well: Take it slow during the test so you have ample time to thoroughly read each passage and respond to all of the questions. Sort questions into tiers of complexity and allot time appropriately.

Writing and Grammar

The CLT's Grammar/Writing component assesses students' proficiency with English grammar, syntax, and use in addition to their ability to write clearly and concisely. This part includes an essay prompt that calls for a written answer in addition to multiple-choice questions that assess grammar and syntax.

Questions Types:

Grammar and Syntax: Students' comprehension of punctuation, sentence structure, grammar rules, and usage are evaluated by these questions. Examinees may be required to recognize grammatical norms, spot faults in sentences, and select the appropriate form of a word or phrase.

Writing an Essay: Students are given a topic or issue to write about and are expected to organize and cogently explain their ideas or arguments in a well-structured essay. It is expected of students to show that they can effectively create a thesis, substantiate it with evidence, and express it.

Success Techniques:

Review the rules of grammar: Review the fundamentals of grammar, such as sentence construction, verb tenses, pronoun agreement, parts of speech, and punctuation. Practice spotting and fixing frequent grammatical mistakes.

Arrange Your Thoughts: Spend some time outlining your primary ideas and creating a concise thesis statement before you start writing the essay. Make sure that your essay is organized logically, with an introduction, many body paragraphs, and a conclusion.

Give Proof to Back Up Your Claims: Provide explanation, facts, and pertinent instances to back up your claims. To bolster your argument and demonstrate your ideas, use precise facts, instances, and tales.

Edit and Make Changes: Set aside some time at the conclusion to go over and edit your essay for grammatical accuracy, consistency, and clarity. Examine your writing for spelling and grammar mistakes, overall effectiveness, and clarity of expression.

Essay Writing Exercises: Write essays on a range of subjects to hone your writing abilities and expand your capacity for coherent, convincing argumentation.

Reasoning Quantitatively

Students' problem-solving, mathematics, and quantitative reasoning skills are evaluated in the CLT's Quantitative Reasoning portion. Multiple-choice problems covering a range of math disciplines, such as algebra, geometry, and data interpretation, are included in this area.

Questions Types:

Algebra: Tasks involving algebra may involve manipulating algebraic expressions, simplifying expressions, and solving equations and inequalities.

Geometry: Properties of lines, angles, triangles, polygons, circles, and three-dimensional figures can all be included in geometry problems. Calculating area, perimeter, volume, and other geometric dimensions may be required of test takers.

Data Interpretation: Students are given tables, graphs, charts, and other visual data representations in data interpretation problems. Examinees are required to understand the data, look for patterns, and make judgments using the information given.

Success Techniques:

Review Core Ideas: Brush up on your knowledge of fundamental math ideas, such as proportions, percentages, ratios, decimals, and arithmetic operations. Establish a solid algebraic and geometrical foundation.

Practice addressing problems: Work on resolving a range of mathematical issues, from easy to difficult. Try out several approaches and methods for addressing problems, such working backwards, creating diagrams, and dissecting difficult issues into manageable chunks.

Recognize the Different Types of Problems: Learn about the kinds of questions that are frequently asked on the CLT, including as geometric puzzles, data analysis tasks, and algebraic equations. In order to guarantee proper interpretation, pay close attention to the language and context of each problem.

Employ scratch paper Use the exam-provided scratch paper to solve math problems, write equations, create diagrams, and arrange your ideas. This will assist you in monitoring your work and preventing thoughtless errors.

Examine your responses: To be sure your responses are accurate and proper, always check them again. Pay close attention to the calculations, units, and mathematical reasoning in particular when reviewing your work.

Morality and Reason

Students' abilities in logical reasoning and ethical reasoning are evaluated in the CLT's Ethics & Logic part. This special section asks students to apply logic and ethical concepts to real-world scenarios through the use of argument analysis questions, logical puzzles, and ethical dilemmas.

Questions Types:

Ethical Dilemmas: These questions pose morally challenging scenarios to students, requiring them to weigh their options, take into account various points of view, and make well-informed ethical decisions. Examinees need to show that they comprehend the moral obligations, ramifications, and ethical concepts.

Logical Puzzles: These kind of problems require the use of thinking and problem-solving techniques, such as pattern recognition, inference, and puzzle solving. To find the right answer, test takers need to employ the concepts of deductive reasoning, logic, and critical thinking.

Argument Analysis: Students are given written arguments or statements to assess for their validity, coherence, and logic in argument analysis problems. Examinees are required to recognize presumptions, recognize logical fallacies, and evaluate the argument's overall validity.

Success Techniques:

Recognize Ethical Principles: Educate oneself on ethical theories and principles, including consequentialism, deontology, virtue ethics, and utilitarianism. When making ethical decisions, take into account the implications, repercussions, and competing moral principles.

Examine scenarios closely: Examine each logical challenge and ethical conundrum thoroughly, taking note of important information, interested parties, and possible outcomes. To make an informed decision, take into account various viewpoints, assess available options, and balance ethical considerations.

Utilize Reasoning Through Logical Application: Apply the concepts of deductive reasoning, logic, and critical thinking to examine assertions, identify assumptions, and analyze arguments. Examine the rationale offered for logical errors, patterns, and contradictions.

Practice Ethical Reasoning: Get comfortable evaluating moral conundrums and rendering moral decisions in a range of situations, including social, professional, and personal ones. To acquire new viewpoints and ideas, discuss ethical scenarios with classmates, teachers, or ethical mentors.

Practice Logical Puzzles: To improve your problem-solving and logical thinking skills, work through a range of logical puzzles and brainteasers. Develop your ability to infer information, reach logical conclusions, and approach puzzle solutions methodically.

In summary

This chapter offers a thorough analysis of every section of the Classic Learning Test (CLT) as well as practical tips for completing it. Completing each area of the test—which includes Verbal Reasoning, Grammar/Writing, Quantitative Reasoning, Ethics & Logic—is necessary to succeed. You can perform to the best of your ability and reach your maximum potential on the CLT by being aware of the subtleties of each segment and using strategic preparation techniques.

Chapter 3: Strategies for Preparation

To succeed on the Classic Learning Test (CLT), preparation is essential. We will examine efficient methods for thoroughly preparing for the test in this chapter. These tips will help you make the most of your study time and improve your performance on exam day. They range from setting realistic goals to making a study timetable and using resources.

Having Reasonable Objectives

Setting attainable goals that fit your abilities and aspirations is crucial before you begin your CLT preparation. Determining precise, attainable goals will provide you direction and drive during your preparation process, regardless of your objectives—improving your critical thinking abilities, reaching a particular score, or getting into a particular school or university.

When you set goals, take into account things like your ultimate objectives, the time you have available for preparation, and your existing level of knowledge and skills. Divide your long-term objectives into smaller, more achievable benchmarks, like finishing practice exams, becoming an expert in a certain subject, or developing your time management abilities. As you strive to succeed on the CLT, you may maintain concentration and motivation by setting reasonable goals and monitoring your progress.

Making a Timetable for Studying

Good time management is necessary to prepare for the CLT successfully. To optimize your time and guarantee steady advancement towards your objectives, design a study plan that harmonizes your scholastic, extracurricular, and personal responsibilities.

To begin, evaluate your existing calendar and mark down time slots that you can use for CLT preparation. Set out specified times to review material that needs improvement, practice with past exams and sample questions, study for each segment of the exam, and take pauses to rejuvenate.

When planning your study schedule, be practical and take into account things like your energy levels, ideal study space, and attention span. Divide up your study periods into more manageable, concentrated chunks to keep your attention and prevent exhaustion. To keep things fresh and engaging, add variation to your study regimen by switching between different subjects and activities.

Making Use of Practice Exams and Resources

Practice exams are a crucial part of CLT preparation because they let you get comfortable with the format, organization, and kinds of questions that will be on the test. Make it a priority to finish several timed practice exams in order to increase your exam endurance and replicate the real examination environment.

Use a range of study tools in addition to practice exams to improve your readiness. Review books, study aids, online courses, educational films, flashcards, and other resources catered to the particular subject topics addressed on the CLT may fall under this category. To strengthen your comprehension of important topics, add extra practice exercises and drills to your study regimen and select resources that suit your learning preferences and style.

To get individualized instruction and progress reports, think about signing up for a test preparation course or hiring a tutor. These tools can offer insightful analysis, useful tactics, and pointers for enhancing your CLT performance and addressing any areas of vulnerability or concern.

Some Advice for Successful Studying

To optimize your preparation, combine the following tactics and recommendations into your study routine in addition to using practice exams and resources:

Concentrate on Your Weaknesses: Determine your areas of weakness or where you still need to grow, and then invest more time and energy into becoming an expert in those subject areas. Determine your areas of weakness with diagnostic tests and practice activities, then adjust your study schedule appropriately.

Evaluate and Ponder: Continually assess your development and consider your advantages and disadvantages. Make a note of any themes or patterns in your work and modify your study techniques accordingly. Take the initiative to address your areas of weakness and, if necessary, seek out further resources or assistance.

Remain Organized: Make sure all of your resources, notes, and study materials are readily available and arranged. Establish a dedicated study area free from distractions so that you may concentrate on your planning. Keep track of your accomplishments and maintain organization by using tools like calendars, planners, and to-do lists.

Take pauses: To relax and rejuvenate, schedule regular pauses within your study schedule. In between study sessions, taking brief breaks can help keep focus and productivity high and prevent burnout. Take use of your breaks to unwind with things like going for a walk, listening to music, or doing mindfulness exercises.

Remain Consistent: Create a regular study schedule and follow it. Since regular study sessions and steady progress toward your objectives are essential for good learning and retention, make an effort to study consistently. Prioritize quality over quantity during your study sessions and refrain from cramming or overloading yourself with material all at once.

Seek Support: If you run into difficulties or need help with your preparation, don't be afraid to ask professors, peers, or mentors for help. To share ideas, pose questions, and get input from others, work with study groups, participate in online forums or discussion groups, and attend review sessions.

Controlling Test Anxiety

Finally, it's critical to deal with test anxiety and create plans for handling tension and anxiety on exam day. It's critical to develop strategies for lowering test anxiety and encouraging a composed, concentrated mentality because test anxiety can have a detrimental effect on performance and prevent you from giving your best on the CLT.

To soothe your anxiety and lower your stress levels, try deep breathing, gradual muscle relaxation, and visualization. Create a pre-test regimen that consists of things that will assist you in feeling at ease and confident, such mindfulness exercises, music listening, or light exercise.

Remind yourself of your preparation and hard work leading up to the test, and picture yourself succeeding and getting good results. Rather than thinking about the result or the fallout in the future, keep your focus on the activity at hand and the present now.

Lastly, keep an optimistic outlook both during your study period and on test day. Instead than viewing the exam as a cause for concern or terror, view it as a chance to demonstrate your talents. You'll be well-prepared to confidently face the CLT if you have faith in your preparation and your capacity to achieve.

In conclusion, meticulous planning, commitment, and the wise use of resources are necessary for successful CLT preparation. You can make the most of your study time and test-day performance by establishing realistic goals, making a study timetable, using resources and practice exams, using efficient study techniques, and controlling test anxiety. You'll be ready to take on the CLT and reach your goals if you have the correct attitude, diligence, and persistence.

Chapter 4: Tests and Practice Questions

There's no greater example of practice making perfect than when it comes to getting ready for the Classic Learning Test (CLT). This chapter will discuss the value of practice tests and questions for CLT preparation, as well as practical methods for making the most of them to improve your performance on test day.

The Value of Application

Exams and practice questions are essential components of CLT preparation since they provide you the chance to become familiar with the format, organization, and kinds of questions you'll see on the test. You can develop your abilities, boost your confidence, and pinpoint any areas of weakness that need further work by practicing on a regular basis.

By allowing you to apply the ideas and techniques you've studied in your study materials to actual situations, practice questions help you better understand and remember important topics. Practice exams can help you create test-taking methods, increase your endurance, and learn good time management techniques by simulating the real testing environment.

Practice Question Types

All of the exam's parts have a variety of themes and question formats covered in CLT practice problems. These could consist of:

Verbal thinking: Critical thinking problems, textual analysis tasks, and reading comprehension passages with questions attached.
Grammar/Writing: Writing exercises, essay prompts, and questions on grammar and syntax.
Math questions involving algebra, geometry, quantitative reasoning, and data interpretation are included in this section.
Logic & Ethics: Argument analysis questions, logical riddles, and ethical dilemma scenarios.

Every kind of practice question is made to evaluate particular competencies that are pertinent to the CLT, enabling you to identify your areas of weakness and adjust the direction of your study.

Techniques for Utilizing Tests and Practice Questions

Take into account the following techniques to maximize the use of practice questions and exams in your CLT preparation:

Start Early: As soon as you can throughout your preparation, start using CLT-style questions for practice. This will allow you plenty of time to get acquainted with the structure and kinds of questions, pinpoint your areas of strength and weakness, and fill up any knowledge gaps.

Concentrate on Quality Rather Than Quantity: How well you interact with practice questions is more important than the number of them you finish. Instead of just learning methods or answers by heart, concentrate on comprehending the underlying ideas and logic of each inquiry.

Review Answers Carefully: Spend some time going over your answers one last time after finishing each practice question or exam. Examine your work, noting any errors or weak points, and consider the logic underlying the right and wrong responses. In the long run, this will help you see trends, solidify your comprehension of important ideas, and perform better.

Simulate Testing Conditions: Try to replicate the real testing environment as much as you can when taking practice tests. To replicate the exam's time limits, set a timer and locate a peaceful, distraction-free workspace. This will assist you in creating test-taking methods, increasing your endurance, and efficiently using your time on test day.

Monitor Your Development: Over time, keep an eye on how well you perform on practice questions and assessments. Make a note of your progress as well as your areas of ongoing difficulty. Utilize this data to modify your study schedule, concentrate on your areas of weakness, and track your advancement toward your objectives.

Request Feedback: If at all feasible, ask peers, teachers, or tutors for their opinions on your practice questions and tests. They can offer insightful commentary, point out areas in need of development, and make recommendations for improving your strategy. Never be afraid to clarify any concepts or tactics you're having trouble with with a question.

Extra Materials

You can enhance your CLT preparation with a range of extra resources in addition to practice problems and exams:

Review Books: All-inclusive review books that go over every topic on the CLT might offer more practice questions, clarifications, and effective study techniques.

Online Resources: Practice questions, study aids, and interactive tools to improve your understanding are abundant on websites, forums, and online groups devoted to CLT preparation.

Tutoring Services: Working with a certified tutor can offer you individualized guidance, constructive criticism, and support based on your unique requirements and learning preferences.

Study Groups: Assembling or starting a study group with peers can offer chances for conversation and learning in a collaborative setting, as well as accountability and incentive.

Official CLT Resources: To aid with your exam preparation, the official CLT website provides practice exams, sample questions, and other materials.

In summary

Effective CLT preparation must include practice questions and examinations, which give you invaluable chances to solidify your grasp of important ideas, hone your test-taking techniques, and track your advancement toward your objectives. You can get the most out of your study sessions and perform at your best on test day by working through practice questions on a regular basis, going over your answers in detail, creating an environment similar to the testing environment, keeping track of your progress, and using extra resources as needed. With commitment, tenacity, and strategic preparation, you'll be ready to overcome the CLT and accomplish your goals.

Chapter 5: Extra Sources

We'll look at a range of extra resources in this chapter that will help you prepare better for the Classic Learning Test (CLT). These options, which range from study groups and tutoring services to review books and internet tools, provide helpful support and direction to improve your CLT preparation process.

Evaluate Books

Thorough review books are excellent tools for CLT preparation since they give you detailed information on the exam's subject matter as well as practice questions, solutions, and success tactics. Every component of the CLT has a review book available, so you may concentrate on your weak points or better direct your preparation efforts.

Look for a review book that complements your learning style, interests, and areas of concentration. Take into account elements like the publisher's or author's repute, the practice questions' quality, and the explanations' lucidity. Popular CLT review books include the following:

Online Resources: "Cracking the CLT" by The Princeton Review; "The Official CLT Study Guide" by Classic Learning Test; "CLT Exam Prep 2024-2025" by Kaplan Test Prep; "CLT Prep Black Book" by Mike Barrett

A plethora of tools, like as blogs, forums, and online communities devoted to standardized testing and college admissions, are available on the internet to help with CLT preparation. You can improve your learning experience by using the interactive tools, study guides, instructional videos, and practice questions that are available through these online resources.

Several well-liked internet resources for getting ready for CLT include:

Official CLT Website: To aid with your exam preparation, the official CLT website provides study guides, practice exams, sample questions, and other materials. Additionally, details regarding test dates, enrollment, and scoring guidelines are available.

Khan Academy: This website provides free online resources such as practice questions, instructional videos, and personalized learning tools for reviewing arithmetic and grammar. You may enhance your confidence in areas where you need it most and brush up on your skills with the aid of these tools.

College Confidential: College Confidential is an online discussion forum where parents, educators, and students talk about standardized testing, college applications, and other matters pertaining to higher education. It's possible to get insightful information, counsel, and encouragement from others who are either taking or have previously taken the CLT.

Reddit: Reddit is home to a number of forums focused on college admissions and standardized testing, such as r/ApplyingToCollege, r/SAT, and r/ACT. These discussion boards offer a space for exchanging study advice, posing queries, and establishing connections with other applicants to colleges.

PrepScholar: This website provides a range of online tools, including as study guides, practice questions, and tutoring services, to help students get ready for standardized tests. In order to assist you in organizing and carrying out your CLT preparation plan, their website also offers articles, tutorials, and resources.

Tutoring Facilities

Engaging with a certified tutor can offer you individualized guidance, constructive criticism, and assistance based on your unique requirements and preferred method of learning. Tutors can assist you in pinpointing your areas of weakness, creating efficient study plans, and boosting your self-assurance.

Look for a tutor with a successful track record and experience instructing CLT preparation before making your selection. Take into account elements including their experience, style of instruction, availability, and price. For the convenience of your schedule and preferences, several tutoring services provide both in-person and online choices.

Several well-liked coaching providers for CLT training consist of:

Varsity Tutors: Varsity Tutors provides one-on-one instruction for the CLT as well as other standardized assessments. To guarantee they are qualified to offer helpful guidance and support, their tutors go through extensive training and evaluation.

Tutor.com: Students of all ages and ability levels can access on-demand tutoring services with Tutor.com. For aid with homework, academic support in other topics, and CLT preparation, you can get in touch with a trained tutor around-the-clock.

Wyzant: Tutors providing individualized tuition in a variety of areas, including CLT preparation, may be found on Wyzant, an online marketplace. You can compare tutors, peruse evaluations, and arrange appointments at your convenience.

Princeton Review: The Princeton Review provides standardized test tutoring, which includes CLT tutoring. With individualized instruction and support, their highly qualified and experienced tutors assist students in reaching their academic objectives.

Study Teams

Forming or joining a study group with peers can offer chances for collaborative learning and discussion, accountability, and inspiration. Study groups provide you the chance to collaborate on difficult concepts, share resources, ask questions, and discuss ideas.

Seek out colleagues who share your goals and aspirations and who are dedicated to preparing for the CLT when organizing study groups. Establish clear expectations and objectives for your study sessions, as well as a convenient time and place for meetings.

Here are some pointers for productive study groups:

Establish a schedule: Every study session should be planned with a clear agenda and objectives in mind. Aim to cover particular subjects or practice questions, and set aside time for review, discussion, and feedback.

Remain Organized: Make sure all of your resources, notes, and study materials are readily available and arranged. To share resources, work together on papers, and monitor progress, create a shared Dropbox or Google Drive folder.

Take Turns Leading: Assign responsibilities to the group's leadership positions so that each member has a chance to participate and assume responsibility for the study process. Assign responsibilities like facilitating talks, providing answers to sample questions, and setting up study materials.

Promote Participation: Motivate everyone in the group to actively participate and engage. Inquire, get feedback, and create a welcoming, encouraging environment where all students feel free to participate.

Review Often: Give yourself some time to evaluate how you're doing and how well your study group is working. To make sure you're getting the most out of your study sessions, evaluate what's going well and where you can improve, then make the necessary adjustments.

In summary

In addition to your own preparation efforts, other tools like study groups, tutoring services, online resources, and review books can offer invaluable help and direction throughout the process. You may boost your comprehension of important ideas, hone your exam-taking techniques, and achieve your best on the CLT by making good use of these tools. You'll be well-prepared to meet your goals on test day and beyond with commitment, tenacity, and the tactical application of extra resources.

Chapter 6: Advice for Exam Day

Test day can be a stressful event, but you can approach the Classic Learning Test (CLT) with calm and confidence if you prepare well and have the correct attitude. This chapter will cover a range of test-day strategies to help you perform at your best and accomplish your goals.

Getting Ready for the Test Day

Examine Test Day Procedures: Become familiar with the policies regarding testing, needed identification, check-in times, and permissible materials. Preparing ahead of time can reduce tension and guarantee a seamless exam day experience.

Assemble Necessary Materials: Get ready everything you'll need ahead of time, such as your admittance ticket, a valid form of identification from the government, #2 or mechanical pencils, erasers, and, if permitted, an authorized calculator. If you want to minimize last-minute stress on test day, pack your luggage the night before.

Get a Good Night's Sleep: To feel alert and rejuvenated on test day, make sure you get a good night's sleep the night before. To aid maximize cognitive performance and focus throughout the exam, try to get at least 7-8 hours of sleep.

Eat a Nutritious meal: To fuel your brain and maintain energy levels throughout the exam, start your day with a nutritious meal that includes complex carbohydrates, protein, and healthy fats. Steer clear of heavy or sugary items that could upset your stomach or induce energy slumps.

Plan Your Route: Organize your travel to the testing facility ahead of time, taking into account things like traffic, parking availability, and public transportation timetables. To allow time for check-in and orientation, try to arrive at least thirty minutes in advance.

Techniques for the Test

Remain Calm and Concentrated: Throughout the test, keep your composure and concentration. Inhale deeply and remind yourself of your readiness and skills. Refrain from obsessing over challenging queries or being agitated by time limits.

study Instructions properly: Before beginning each exam segment, give yourself enough time to properly study the instructions and procedures. Be mindful of any unique needs or limitations, like time limits or restrictions on using a calculator.

Use Your Time Sensibly: Take it slow during the test to make sure you have enough time to finish each part and go over your responses. Don't spend too much time on any one question; instead, carefully allocate your time according to the quantity and difficulty of the questions.

Answer Every Question: Even if you're not confident of the right answer, make sure to respond to every question on the test. It is preferable to guess rather than to leave a question blank because there is no penalty for doing so.

Ignore Tough Questions: If a question seems especially difficult, don't give up. If you have time, skip it and go on to the next question. If not, come back to it later. Starting with the simpler questions can help you gain confidence and enthusiasm.

Employ the Process of Elimination: To reduce your possibilities and arrive at a well-informed guess when you are unsure of the answer, apply the process of elimination. After removing any selections that are blatantly erroneous, carefully weigh the options that remain before choosing.

Strategies for After Exams

Examine Your Responses: Before submitting your exam, if time permits, carefully go over your responses. Make any required edits or modifications after checking for any mistakes or omissions. Have faith in your intuition, but also be prepared to reevaluate your responses if you are unsure.

Remain Positive: No matter how you think the test went, keep a positive outlook on things. Rather than focusing on apparent flaws or errors, concentrate on what you did well and the preparation you put in.

After the exam is finished, take some time to recognize and appreciate your efforts and successes. To relax and rejuvenate, treat yourself to a fulfilling activity or indulge in your favorite pastimes.

Examine Your Experience: Consider how you felt on exam day and note any areas where your study or test-taking techniques could be strengthened. To improve your performance, think about what went well and what you would do differently the next time.

After the exam, reflect on your objectives and aspirations and make a plan for your next steps. Create a plan of action to carry forth your academic journey with confidence and tenacity, regardless of whether you're happy with your results or hoping to repeat the exam.

In summary

Test day can be both difficult and rewarding, and you can ace the Classic Learning Test (CLT) with poise and confidence if you prepare well and have the appropriate attitude. You can optimize your performance, reduce stress, and accomplish your goals by using these test-day techniques and recommendations. Remain composed, maintain your attention, and have faith in your planning and skills. On exam day and beyond, you'll be well-prepared with commitment, tenacity, and a positive outlook.

Chapter 7: Complex Methods for Every Area

We will explore advanced strategies in this chapter that are specific to each area of the Classic Learning Test (CLT). These techniques are intended to assist you in honing your abilities, tackling difficult problems, and performing at your best on exam day. Gaining proficiency in these advanced approaches can provide you with a competitive advantage and boost your confidence when taking the CLT. These techniques include verbal reasoning, grammar/writing, mathematical reasoning, ethics & logic, and more.

Improved Methods of Verbal Reasoning

Active Reading Techniques: Use active reading techniques to improve your ability to understand and remember material. This entails noting important details, highlighting the major concepts, and determining the tone and viewpoint of the author. Analyze the material critically by challenging presumptions, assessing the available data, and speculating on the author's point of view.

Prioritize passages according to their length and intricacy via strategic passage selection. Once you're warmed up, start with shorter, easier passages to gain momentum and confidence before moving on to longer or more difficult ones. Make sure you have enough time to read each passage and respond to the questions by carefully planning your schedule.

Pre-reading Questions: Examine the accompanying questions to find important ideas or details to pay attention to while reading a piece before delving into it. This can assist you in concentrating your attention and directing your reading comprehension efforts, resulting in more correct and timely responses.

Contextual Inference: Develop your skill of contextual inference by interpreting unknown words or phrases based on surrounding context. To determine the intended meaning of ambiguous expressions, pay attention to contextual cues including tone, syntax, and adjacent sentences.

Evidence-Based Reasoning: When responding to inquiries, use evidence-based reasoning by consulting the passage again for clarification. To support your answers and keep yourself from slipping into the traps set by detractors, avoid depending only on gut feeling or past knowledge. Instead, give priority to the evidence that is explicitly mentioned in the text.

Advanced Writing and Grammar Techniques

Sentence Structure Analysis: Acquire an acute understanding of sentence structure by recognizing grammatical components like parallelism, subject-verb agreement, and modifiers. Deconstruct complex phrases into their component pieces in order to better spot faults and explain meaning.

Precision in Language usage: Practice precision in language usage by choosing words and phrases that best express the meaning you want to get across. When selecting vocabulary, consider tone, context, and implications. Stay clear of ambiguity and vagueness in your writing.

Transitional Phrases and Cohesion: provide your writing more coherent and cohesive by employing logical connectors and transitional phrases to connect concepts and provide seamless transitions between sentences and paragraphs. This makes your writing easier to read and aids in directing the reader through your story or argument.

Structural Organization: Give your articles a coherent, logical order with a compelling introduction, well-developed body paragraphs, and a succinct conclusion. To keep coherence, use topic sentences to introduce each paragraph's major point and make sure the ideas flow naturally amongst one another.

Develop your editing and revising techniques to polish your writing and get rid of mistakes. Check your essays for correct grammar, coherence of argument, and clarity of speech. When editing your writing, take into account elements like sentence structure, punctuation, word choice, and general coherence.

More Complex Methods of Quantitative Reasoning

Approaches to Strategic Problem-Solving: To effectively solve challenging arithmetic issues, cultivate strategic methods to problem-solving. Before beginning any computations, break down multi-step problems into manageable components, find pertinent information, and create an attack strategy.

Alternative Approaches to Solving Problems: Examine several approaches to solving problems outside the conventional ones, like employing pictorial aids, manipulating algebra, or applying logic. Try out many approaches to identify the most elegant and effective answer for every issue.

Data Interpretation Skills: Practice interpreting a range of charts, graphs, tables, and other visual data representations to hone your skills. Acquire the ability to extract pertinent data, recognize patterns and trends, and make inferences from the data provided.

Calculator Optimization: Learn how to use your calculator to complete tasks more quickly and precisely. Learn about its features and functions, and get comfortable with employing shortcuts and time-saving techniques to speed up calculations and reduce exam time.

Backsolving and Plugging In: Use these strategies to cross-check your answers and validate solutions. To evaluate alternative answers and rule out wrong options, move backwards from the answer choices or plug in values instead of solving problems algebraically from start to finish.

Sophisticated Methods for Logic and Ethics

Principled Decision Making: By basing your decisions on core moral principles and values, you can cultivate a principled approach to making ethical decisions. Think on the moral ramifications and effects of different choices, and make an effort to behave morally—that is, with justice, fairness, and integrity in mind.

Logic Fallacies, syllogisms, conditional assertions, deductive and inductive reasoning, and other typical logical thinking patterns should be understood. Develop your ability to recognize and evaluate these patterns in logical problems, ethical quandaries, and debates.

Analysis of Counterarguments: When assessing arguments or moral quandaries, hone your analytical abilities by taking into account counterarguments and other viewpoints. Before coming to a well-reasoned conclusion, consider the advantages and disadvantages of many points of view and be prepared for any possible objections or criticisms.

Critical Thinking Exercises: Practice critical thinking to strengthen your analytical and reasoning skills. Practice analyzing the facts, spotting biases, and determining the veracity of arguments in a range of settings, from casual discussions to scholarly debates.

Debate and Discussion: To hone your argumentative abilities and interact with ethical concerns from a variety of angles, take part in debates, discussions, or simulated trials. Work together with peers to assess opposing viewpoints, analyze difficult ethical conundrums, and come at well-informed decisions through reasoned discussion.

In summary

It takes effort, practice, and perseverance to master advanced approaches for every area of the Classic Learning Test (CLT) and to continuously progress. You may hone your abilities, increase your self-assurance, and perform to the best of your ability on exam day by using these tactics in your preparation. Whether your focus is on verbal reasoning, grammar/writing, quantitative reasoning, ethics & logic, or any other area, these advanced strategies will enable you to get over obstacles, work through challenging questions, and succeed on the CLT. By practicing these strategies consistently and using them strategically, you'll be ready to do well on the test and demonstrate your skills with accuracy and clarity.

Chapter 8: Specific Skill Development

We'll look at specific skill improvement tactics in this chapter to help you do better on the Classic Learning Test (CLT). These focused strategies can assist you in addressing particular areas of weakness and achieving your desired results on test day, whether your goal is to improve your reading comprehension, your mathematics skills, or your critical thinking ability.

Determining Weakness Areas

Diagnostic Evaluation: To start, carry out a diagnostic evaluation to pinpoint your areas of strength and need. Examine your past performance on practice exams and questions, noting any tendencies toward mistakes or question types that you find difficult.

Self-Reflection: Consider your intellectual and cognitive strengths and shortcomings. Take into account things like your time management techniques, critical thinking capabilities, mathematical aptitude, and reading comprehension ability. Determine the precise areas in which you lack confidence or competence, and give them top priority so that you may make targeted improvements.

Examine Practice Test Feedback: Examine practice test feedback, highlighting questions that were missed, wrong answers, and areas of uncertainty. Examine the justifications provided for inaccurate answers, and note any recurrent themes or widespread misunderstandings that might be impeding your performance.

Specific Methods for Enhancement

Understanding What You Read

Practice active reading strategies by making annotations on sections, summarizing the main points, and pointing out important features and supporting data.
Increase the breadth of your vocabulary by reading widely on a variety of subjects and genres. As you learn new terms and their definitions, write them

down in a vocabulary notebook and use them in your regular writing and reading exercises.

Work on Complicated Texts: Read more difficult and sophisticated literature, such as philosophy essays, historical accounts, scientific articles, and literary fiction, to push oneself. To improve your understanding and analytical abilities, pay close attention to the author's tone, arguments, and use of rhetorical devices.

Proficiency in Mathematics

Conceptual Understanding: Put a lot of effort into developing a solid conceptual grasp of mathematical ideas and methods. Examine basic subjects like geometry, algebra, arithmetic, and data analysis, and then practice using these ideas to solve issues in various situations.

Techniques for Solving Problems: Develop tactics for solving difficulties, such as dividing issues into manageable chunks, finding pertinent information, and selecting suitable approaches. To improve your fluency and confidence in your mathematics skills, practice with a range of problem kinds and levels of complexity.

Utilize Timed Exercises for Practice: To replicate the pressure of a test, practice answering arithmetic problems in a timed environment. Put efficiency and precision first, and give priority to tactics that will help you move forward steadily and reduce mistakes in the allocated amount of time.

Analytical reasoning and critical thinking

Practice evaluating arguments for their underlying assumptions, logical flow, and validity. Seek proof, assess logic, and point out any logical errors or inconsistencies in the argument.

Ethical problems and Logical Puzzles: Work on your critical thinking and ethical reasoning skills by solving logical puzzles and ethical problems. Examine opposing viewpoints, balance conflicting moral principles, and assess the effects of various options.

Debate and Discussion: To engage with complicated subjects from different perspectives, take part in debates, discussions, or critical thinking exercises. Develop your ability to present your own arguments, defend your viewpoint, and refute opponents' points of view in a logical and convincing way.

Putting Targeted Practice into Practice

concentrated Study Sessions: Set aside time for concentrated study sessions to concentrate on improving one particular ability at a time. Prioritize practice exercises and activities that correspond with your areas of weakness and establish clear goals and objectives for each session.

Progress tracking: Keep tabs on your development over time by keeping score on tests, quizzes, and practice questions. Record your results, the amount of time it took, and your areas for growth. Then, using your strengths and shortcomings as a guide, modify your study schedule.

Adaptive Learning Tools: Make use of resources and tools that are customized to your unique requirements and learning preferences. Investigate web resources, mobile applications, and software that provide tailored study suggestions, adaptive practice tasks, and individualised feedback depending on your performance.

Feedback and reflection: Get input on your performance and growth from peers, teachers, or tutors. To improve your study techniques over time, evaluate your strengths and places for growth and include feedback into your routine.

In summary

Achieving your intended results on test day and optimizing your performance on the Classic Learning Test (CLT) need targeted skill improvement. You can increase your reading comprehension, math competency, critical thinking skills, and general test-taking ability by pinpointing your areas of weakness, putting focused practice into action, and applying targeted improvement tactics. You may succeed on exam day and approach the CLT with confidence if you have commitment, perseverance, and a deliberate approach to focused skill development.

Practice Questions and Answers Explanations 2024-2025

Question 1:
Which of the following is an example of an ethical dilemma?
A) Choosing between attending two equally important events
B) Deciding whether to cheat on a test
C) Selecting a college major based on personal interests
D) Determining whether to report a coworker for unethical behavior

Answer: D) Determining whether to report a coworker for unethical behavior

Explanation: An ethical dilemma involves choosing between two conflicting moral principles or courses of action, often with no clear right or wrong answer. Reporting a coworker for unethical behavior presents a moral dilemma because it requires weighing the ethical obligation to uphold integrity against potential consequences for the coworker.

Question 2:
In the sentence "The cat sat on the mat," which word is the subject?
A) The
B) Cat
C) Sat
D) Mat

Answer: B) Cat

Explanation: In English grammar, the subject of a sentence is the noun or pronoun that performs the action of the verb. In this sentence, "cat" is the subject because it is the noun performing the action of sitting.

Question 3:
What is the value of x in the equation $2x + 5 = 15$?
A) 5
B) 7
C) 8
D) 10

Answer: C) 8

Explanation: To solve for x, first subtract 5 from both sides of the equation: $2x = 15 - 5 = 10$. Then, divide both sides by 2 to isolate x: $x = 10 / 2 = 5$.

Question 4:
Which of the following statements accurately describes the setting of a story?
A) The main character's internal thoughts and feelings
B) The sequence of events in the plot
C) The physical environment and time period in which the story takes place
D) The conflict between characters or forces in the story

Answer: C) The physical environment and time period in which the story takes place

Explanation: The setting of a story refers to the physical environment, time period, and geographical location in which the events of the narrative occur. It provides context for the plot and influences the actions and experiences of the characters.

Question 5:
What is the main purpose of a thesis statement in an essay?
A) To summarize the main points of the essay
B) To present the author's argument or claim
C) To provide background information on the topic
D) To offer a counterargument to opposing viewpoints

Answer: B) To present the author's argument or claim

Explanation: A thesis statement is a concise statement that presents the main argument or claim of an essay. It serves as a roadmap for the reader, guiding the direction of the essay and indicating the author's stance on the topic.

Question 6:
What is the square root of 64?
A) 4
B) 8
C) 16
D) 32

Answer: B) 8

Explanation: The square root of a number is a value that, when multiplied by itself, equals the original number. Therefore, the square root of 64 is 8 because 8 * 8 = 64.

Question 7:
Which of the following terms refers to the repetition of consonant sounds at the beginning of words in close proximity?
A) Alliteration
B) Metaphor
C) Simile
D) Personification

Answer: A) Alliteration

Explanation: Alliteration is a literary device that involves the repetition of consonant sounds at the beginning of words in close proximity. It is often used for emphasis, rhythm, or poetic effect in writing and speech.

Question 8:
What is the capital of France?
A) Rome
B) Madrid
C) Paris
D) Berlin

Answer: C) Paris

Explanation: Paris is the capital city of France, known for its iconic landmarks such as the Eiffel Tower, Louvre Museum, and Notre-Dame Cathedral.

Question 9:
Which of the following is an example of an adverb?
A) Dog
B) Run
C) Quickly
D) Blue

Answer: C) Quickly

Explanation: An adverb is a word that modifies a verb, adjective, or other adverb, often indicating manner, time, place, degree, or frequency. "Quickly" is an adverb that modifies the verb "run."

Question 10:
What is the sum of 5 and 7?
A) 9
B) 10
C) 11
D) 12

Answer: D) 12

Explanation: To find the sum of 5 and 7, simply add the two numbers together: 5 + 7 = 12.

Question 11:
In the sentence "Sheila baked cookies and cakes for the party," which word is a coordinating conjunction?
A) Sheila
B) Baked
C) Cookies
D) And

Answer: D) And

Explanation: A coordinating conjunction is a word that connects words, phrases, or clauses of equal grammatical rank. In this sentence, "and" is a coordinating conjunction that joins the nouns "cookies" and "cakes."

Question 12:
Who wrote the play "Romeo and Juliet"?
A) William Shakespeare
B) Jane Austen
C) Charles Dickens
D) F. Scott Fitzgerald

Answer: A) William Shakespeare

Explanation: "Romeo and Juliet" is a tragedy written by William Shakespeare, one of the most renowned playwrights in English literature.

Question 13:
Which of the following literary devices involves the repetition of vowel sounds within words in close proximity?
A) Alliteration
B) Assonance
C) Onomatopoeia
D) Hyperbole

Answer: B) Assonance

Explanation: Assonance is a literary device that involves the repetition of vowel sounds within words in close proximity. It is often used for musical or rhythmic effect in poetry and prose.

Question 14:
What is the product of 9 and 8?
A) 16
B) 63
C) 72
D) 81

Answer: C) 72

Explanation: To find the product of 9 and 8, simply multiply the two numbers together: 9 * 8 = 72.

Question 15:
Which of the following sentences is written in the passive voice?
A) The teacher assigned the homework.
B) The homework was assigned by the teacher.
C) The students completed the assignment quickly.
D) We will finish the project tomorrow.

Answer: B) The homework was assigned by the teacher.

Explanation: The passive voice occurs when the subject of the sentence is acted upon by the verb. In this sentence, "the homework" is the subject being acted upon by the verb "was assigned."

Question 16:
Who is the protagonist in the novel "To Kill a Mockingbird"?
A) Atticus Finch
B) Scout Finch
C) Boo Radley
D) Tom Robinson

Answer: B) Scout Finch

Explanation: Scout Finch is the protagonist and narrator of Harper Lee's novel "To Kill a Mockingbird," which follows her coming-of-age journey in the racially charged setting of the American South.

Question 17:
What is the capital of Japan?
A) Seoul
B) Beijing
C) Tokyo
D) Bangkok

Answer: C) Tokyo

Explanation: Tokyo is the capital city of Japan, known for its vibrant culture, advanced technology, and bustling cityscape.

Question 18:
Which of the following is an example of a simile?
A) The stars winked in the night sky.
B) The wind whispered through the trees.
C) Her smile was as bright as the sun.
D) Time flies when you're having fun.

Answer: C) Her smile was as bright as the sun.

Explanation: A simile is a figure of speech that compares two unlike things using the words "like" or "as." In this sentence, "as bright as the sun" is a simile comparing the brightness of the smile to the sun.

Question 19:
What is the next number in the sequence: 1, 1, 2, 3, 5, 8, ...?
A) 10
B) 11
C) 13
D) 21

Answer: C) 13

Explanation: The sequence follows the Fibonacci sequence, where each number is the sum of the two preceding ones. Therefore, the next number is 8 + 5 = 13.

Question 20:
Who is the author of "The Great Gatsby"?
A) F. Scott Fitzgerald
B) Ernest Hemingway
C) Mark Twain
D) J.D. Salinger

Answer: A) F. Scott Fitzgerald

Explanation: "The Great Gatsby" is a novel written by F. Scott Fitzgerald, depicting the Jazz Age and exploring themes of wealth, love, and the American Dream.

Question 21:
What is the plural form of "child"?
A) Childs
B) Childes
C) Children
D) Childs'

Answer: C) Children

Explanation: The plural form of "child" is "children," with the addition of the "-ren" suffix to indicate multiple individuals.

Question 22:
Which of the following terms refers to a comparison between two unlike things without using "like" or "as"?
A) Metaphor
B) Simile
C) Personification
D) Hyperbole

Answer: A) Metaphor

Explanation: A metaphor is a figure of speech that compares two unlike things by stating that one thing is another. Unlike a simile, it does not use "like" or "as" to make the comparison explicit.

Question 23:
What is the sum of the interior angles of a triangle?
A) 90 degrees
B) 180 degrees
C) 270 degrees
D) 360 degrees

Answer: B) 180 degrees

Explanation: The sum of the interior angles of any triangle is always 180 degrees, regardless of the triangle's size or shape.

Question 24:
Who wrote the novel "Pride and Prejudice"?
A) Jane Austen
B) Emily Brontë
C) Charlotte Brontë
D) George Eliot

Answer: A) Jane Austen

Explanation: "Pride and Prejudice" is a novel written by Jane Austen, one of the most celebrated authors of English literature.

Question 25:
Which of the following terms refers to the main idea or central message of a literary work?
A) Theme
B) Plot
C) Characterization
D) Setting

Answer: A) Theme

Explanation: The theme of a literary work is the underlying message or central idea that the author explores through the narrative. It often reflects universal truths or insights about human nature, society, or the human condition.

Question 26:
What is the capital of Australia?
A) Sydney
B) Melbourne
C) Canberra
D) Brisbane

Answer: C) Canberra

Explanation: Canberra is the capital city of Australia, located in the Australian Capital Territory. It serves as the seat of the Australian government and houses important institutions such as Parliament House.

Question 27:
Who is the author of the play "Hamlet"?
A) William Shakespeare
B) George Bernard Shaw
C) Christopher Marlowe
D) Tennessee Williams

Answer: A) William Shakespeare

Explanation: "Hamlet" is a tragedy written by William Shakespeare, considered one of his greatest works and one of the most influential plays in English literature.

Question 28:
What is the chemical symbol for gold?
A) Au
B) Ag
C) Fe
D) Pb

Answer: A) Au

Explanation: The chemical symbol for gold is Au, derived from the Latin word "aurum."

Question 29:
Which of the following is a renewable energy source?
A) Coal
B) Natural Gas
C) Solar
D) Petroleum

Answer: C) Solar

Explanation: Solar energy is a renewable energy source derived from the sun's radiation, which can be converted into electricity using photovoltaic cells or concentrated solar power systems.

Question 30:
In the sentence "The sun sets in the west," which word is the predicate?
A) The
B) Sun
C) Sets
D) West

Answer: C) Sets

Explanation: In English grammar, the predicate of a sentence is the part that expresses the action or state of being. In this sentence, "sets" is the predicate, indicating the action of the sun.

Question 31:
Who wrote the novel "1984"?
A) George Orwell
B) Aldous Huxley
C) Ray Bradbury
D) Margaret Atwood

Answer: A) George Orwell

Explanation: "1984" is a dystopian novel written by George Orwell, exploring themes of totalitarianism, surveillance, and government oppression.

Question 32:
Which of the following terms refers to a figure of speech that attributes human qualities or characteristics to inanimate objects or abstract concepts?
A) Simile
B) Metaphor
C) Personification
D) Hyperbole

Answer: C) Personification

Explanation: Personification is a literary device that gives human traits or attributes to non-human entities, enhancing the vividness and emotional impact of the writing.

Question 33:
What is the capital of Brazil?
A) Brasília
B) Rio de Janeiro
C) São Paulo
D) Salvador

Answer: A) Brasília

Explanation: Brasília is the capital city of Brazil, known for its modernist architecture and status as a UNESCO World Heritage Site.

Question 34:
Which of the following terms refers to a word that has the opposite meaning of another word?
A) Synonym
B) Antonym
C) Homonym
D) Homophone

Answer: B) Antonym

Explanation: An antonym is a word that has the opposite meaning of another word. For example, "hot" is an antonym of "cold."

Question 35:
What is the formula for calculating the area of a rectangle?
A) Length × Width
B) Length + Width
C) (Length + Width) ÷ 2
D) 2 × (Length + Width)

Answer: A) Length × Width

Explanation: The formula for calculating the area of a rectangle is length multiplied by width. In mathematical notation, it is often represented as A = l × w.

Question 36:
Who wrote the novel "Moby-Dick"?
A) Herman Melville
B) Nathaniel Hawthorne
C) Mark Twain
D) Ralph Waldo Emerson

Answer: A) Herman Melville

Explanation: "Moby-Dick" is a novel written by Herman Melville, depicting the obsessive quest of Captain Ahab for the white whale Moby Dick.

Question 37:
Which of the following elements is a noble gas?
A) Helium
B) Sodium
C) Oxygen
D) Carbon

Answer: A) Helium

Explanation: Helium is a noble gas, known for its inertness and stability. It is commonly used in balloons, airships, and cryogenic applications.

Question 38:
What is the plural form of "goose"?
A) Goos
B) Geese
C) Goose
D) Gooze

Answer: B) Geese

Explanation: The plural form of "goose" is "geese," with the addition of the "-se" suffix to indicate multiple individuals.

Question 39:
Which of the following terms refers to a word that sounds like the noise it describes?
A) Alliteration
B) Onomatopoeia
C) Assonance
D) Consonance

Answer: B) Onomatopoeia

Explanation: Onomatopoeia is a literary device that uses words to imitate the sounds they represent, such as "buzz," "bang," or "moo."

Question 40:

What is the capital of Italy?

A) Rome

B) Milan

C) Florence

D) Naples

Answer: A) Rome

Explanation: Rome is the capital city of Italy, known for its rich history, iconic landmarks such as the Colosseum and Vatican City, and cultural heritage.

Question 41:

Who composed the famous symphony "Symphony No. 9"?

A) Ludwig van Beethoven

B) Wolfgang Amadeus Mozart

C) Johann Sebastian Bach

D) Franz Schubert

Answer: A) Ludwig van Beethoven

Explanation: "Symphony No. 9," also known as the "Choral Symphony," was composed by Ludwig van Beethoven and is one of the most celebrated works in classical music.

Question 42:

What is the chemical symbol for silver?

A) Si

B) Ag

C) Sn

D) S

Answer: B) Ag

Explanation: The chemical symbol for silver is Ag, derived from the Latin word "argentum."

Question 43:
Which of the following is not a primary color in the RGB color model?
A) Red
B) Green
C) Blue
D) Yellow

Answer: D) Yellow

Explanation: In the RGB color model used in digital displays, the primary colors are red, green, and blue. Yellow is a primary color in subtractive color models such as CMYK used in printing.

Question 44:
Who is the author of the novel "The Catcher in the Rye"?
A) J.D. Salinger
B) Ernest Hemingway
C) F. Scott Fitzgerald
D) John Steinbeck

Answer: A) J.D. Salinger

Explanation: "The Catcher in the Rye" is a novel written by J.D. Salinger, narrated by the disillusioned teenager Holden Caulfield.

Question 45:
What is the square root of 81?
A) 8
B) 9
C) 10
D) 11

Answer: B) 9

Explanation: The square root of 81 is 9, as 9 multiplied by itself equals 81.

Question 46:
Which of the following is an example of a proper noun?
A) book
B) cat
C) New York City
D) table

Answer: C) New York City

Explanation: A proper noun is a specific name used for an individual person, place, or organization. "New York City" is a proper noun because it refers to a specific location.

Question 47:
What is the chemical symbol for water?
A) H2O
B) H2
C) O2
D) HO

Answer: A) H2O

Explanation: The chemical formula for water is H2O, indicating two hydrogen atoms bonded to one oxygen atom.

Question 48:
Who is the author of the novel "Frankenstein"?
A) Mary Shelley
B) Bram Stoker
C) Edgar Allan Poe
D) H.G. Wells

Answer: A) Mary Shelley

Explanation: "Frankenstein; or, The Modern Prometheus" is a novel written by Mary Shelley, depicting the story of scientist Victor Frankenstein and his creation.

Question 49:

What is the capital of South Africa?

A) Johannesburg

B) Pretoria

C) Cape Town

D) Durban

Answer: B) Pretoria

Explanation: Pretoria is one of the three capital cities of South Africa, serving as the administrative capital and home to the government's executive branch.

Question 50:

What is the chemical symbol for carbon?

A) Ca

B) Co

C) Cr

D) C

Answer: D) C

Explanation: The chemical symbol for carbon is C, derived from the Latin word "carbo."

Question 51:

Who wrote the novel "The Adventures of Huckleberry Finn"?

A) Mark Twain

B) Herman Melville

C) Nathaniel Hawthorne

D) Emily Dickinson

Answer: A) Mark Twain

Explanation: "The Adventures of Huckleberry Finn" is a novel written by Mark Twain, following the adventures of the titular character Huck Finn along the Mississippi River.

Question 52:
Which of the following is an example of an oxymoron?
A) Jumbo shrimp
B) Pretty ugly
C) Deafening silence
D) Bitter sweet

Answer: D) Bitter sweet

Explanation: An oxymoron is a figure of speech that combines contradictory terms to create a paradoxical effect. "Bitter sweet" combines the contrasting sensations of bitterness and sweetness.

Question 53:
What is the capital of Spain?
A) Barcelona
B) Seville
C) Madrid
D) Valencia

Answer: C) Madrid

Explanation: Madrid is the capital city of Spain, known for its rich cultural heritage, historic architecture, and vibrant nightlife.

Question 54:
What is the chemical symbol for iron?
A) Ir
B) Fe
C) In
D) Io

Answer: B) Fe

Explanation: The chemical symbol for iron is Fe, derived from the Latin word "ferrum."

Question 55:
What is the next number in the sequence: 1, 4, 9, 16, 25, ...?
A) 30
B) 36
C) 49
D) 64

Answer: D) 64

Explanation: The sequence consists of perfect squares of consecutive natural numbers. Therefore, the next number is 7 squared, which is 49.

Question 56:
Who painted the "Mona Lisa"?
A) Leonardo da Vinci
B) Michelangelo
C) Pablo Picasso
D) Vincent van Gogh

Answer: A) Leonardo da Vinci

Explanation: The "Mona Lisa" is a famous portrait painted by Leonardo da Vinci during the Italian Renaissance.

Question 57:
What is the plural form of "mouse"?
A) Mouses
B) Mice
C) Mice's
D) Mouse's

Answer: B) Mice

Explanation: The plural form of "mouse" is "mice," with the addition of the "-ice" suffix to indicate multiple individuals.

Question 58:
Which of the following terms refers to the sequence of events in a story?
A) Theme
B) Plot
C) Setting
D) Characterization

Answer: B) Plot

Explanation: The plot of a story refers to the sequence of events that make up the narrative, including exposition, rising action, climax, falling action, and resolution.

Question 59:
What is the chemical symbol for sodium?
A) Sa
B) Sn
C) So
D) Na

Answer: D) Na

Explanation: The chemical symbol for sodium is Na, derived from the Latin word "natrium."

Question 60:
Who is the protagonist in the novel "The Great Gatsby"?
A) Jay Gatsby
B) Daisy Buchanan
C) Nick Carraway
D) Tom Buchanan

Answer: C) Nick Carraway

Explanation: Nick Carraway is the narrator and protagonist of "The Great Gatsby," serving as the lens through which the reader experiences the events of the story.

Question 61:
What is the chemical symbol for oxygen?
A) O
B) Ox
C) Oc
D) Oxg

Answer: A) O

Explanation: The chemical symbol for oxygen is O, derived from the Greek word "oxygène."

Question 62:
Which of the following is not a type of cloud?
A) Cirrus
B) Nimbus
C) Stratus
D) Cirque

Answer: D) Cirque

Explanation: A cirque is a geological feature, specifically a bowl-shaped depression formed by glacial erosion. Cirrus, nimbus, and stratus are types of clouds.

Question 63:
Who wrote the play "Macbeth"?
A) William Shakespeare
B) Christopher Marlowe
C) Ben Jonson
D) John Donne

Answer: A) William Shakespeare

Explanation: "Macbeth" is a tragedy written by William Shakespeare, exploring themes of ambition, power, and moral corruption.

Question 64:

Which of the following is not a primary color in the subtractive color model?

A) Cyan
B) Magenta
C) Yellow
D) Black

Answer: D) Black

Explanation: In the subtractive color model used in printing, the primary colors are cyan, magenta, and yellow. Black is added as a fourth color to improve contrast and depth.

Question 65:

What is the capital of China?

A) Shanghai
B) Beijing
C) Guangzhou
D) Shenzhen

Answer: B) Beijing

Explanation: Beijing is the capital city of China, known for its historic landmarks such as the Forbidden City, Temple of Heaven, and Great Wall of China.

Question 66:

Who wrote the novel "Jane Eyre"?

A) Charlotte Brontë
B) Emily Brontë
C) Anne Brontë
D) Jane Austen

Answer: A) Charlotte Brontë

Explanation: "Jane Eyre" is a novel written by Charlotte Brontë, depicting the journey of the titular character from childhood to adulthood and her search for independence and love.

Question 67:
What is the chemical symbol for helium?
A) He
B) H
C) Ha
D) Hy

Answer: A) He

Explanation: The chemical symbol for helium is He, derived from the Greek word "helios."

Question 68:
Which of the following terms refers to the use of humor, irony, or exaggeration to criticize or mock individuals, society, or politics?
A) Satire
B) Parody
C) Sarcasm
D) Irony

Answer: A) Satire

Explanation: Satire is a literary technique that uses humor, irony, or exaggeration to critique and ridicule human folly, vices, or societal norms.

Question 69:
What is the capital of Canada?
A) Toronto
B) Vancouver
C) Ottawa
D) Montreal

Answer: C) Ottawa

Explanation: Ottawa is the capital city of Canada, located in the province of Ontario and serving as the seat of the Canadian government.

Question 70:
Who painted the famous mural "The Last Supper"?
A) Leonardo da Vinci
B) Michelangelo
C) Raphael
D) Sandro Botticelli

Answer: A) Leonardo da Vinci

Explanation: "The Last Supper" is a renowned mural painted by Leonardo da Vinci, depicting the final meal of Jesus Christ with his disciples before his crucifixion.

Question 71:
What is the chemical symbol for potassium?
A) P
B) K
C) Po
D) Pt

Answer: B) K

Explanation: The chemical symbol for potassium is K, derived from the Latin word "kalium."

Question 72:
Which of the following terms refers to the repetition of similar vowel sounds in nearby words?
A) Assonance
B) Alliteration
C) Consonance
D) Onomatopoeia

Answer: A) Assonance

Explanation: Assonance is a literary device that involves the repetition of similar vowel sounds in nearby words, creating a melodic or rhythmic effect in poetry and prose.

Question 73:
What is the plural form of "cactus"?
A) Cacti
B) Cactuses
C) Cactuss
D) Cacteese

Answer: A) Cacti

Explanation: The plural form of "cactus" is "cacti," with the addition of the "-i" suffix to indicate multiple individuals.

Question 74:
Who wrote the play "Romeo and Juliet"?
A) William Shakespeare
B) Christopher Marlowe
C) John Milton
D) Ben Jonson

Answer: A) William Shakespeare

Explanation: "Romeo and Juliet" is a tragedy written by William Shakespeare, depicting the tragic love story of the titular characters from feuding families.

Question 75:
What is the chemical symbol for silver?
A) Ag
B) Au
C) Si
D) Sn

Answer: A) Ag

Explanation: The chemical symbol for silver is Ag, derived from the Latin word "argentum."

Question 76:
Which of the following terms refers to the emotional atmosphere or mood created by a literary work?
A) Tone
B) Theme
C) Atmosphere
D) Style

Answer: C) Atmosphere

Explanation: Atmosphere, also known as mood, refers to the emotional tone or ambiance created by a literary work through descriptions, setting, and language choices.

Question 77:
What is the capital of France?
A) Paris
B) Marseille
C) Lyon
D) Nice

Answer: A) Paris

Explanation: Paris is the capital city of France, known for its iconic landmarks such as the Eiffel Tower, Louvre Museum, and Notre-Dame Cathedral.

Question 78:
Who composed the famous ballet "Swan Lake"?
A) Pyotr Ilyich Tchaikovsky
B) Ludwig van Beethoven
C) Johannes Brahms
D) Frédéric Chopin

Answer: A) Pyotr Ilyich Tchaikovsky

Explanation: "Swan Lake" is a ballet composed by Pyotr Ilyich Tchaikovsky, featuring a tragic love story between Prince Siegfried and Odette, the Swan Queen.

Question 79:
What is the chemical symbol for lead?
A) P
B) L
C) Le
D) Pb

Answer: D) Pb

Explanation: The chemical symbol for lead is Pb, derived from the Latin word "plumbum."

Question 80:
What is the plural form of "ox"?
A) Oxen
B) Oxes
C) Oxs
D) Ox's

Answer: A) Oxen

Explanation: The plural form of "ox" is "oxen," following irregular pluralization rules.

Question 81:
Which of the following terms refers to a sudden and unexpected twist or turn of events in a story?
A) Climax
B) Foreshadowing
C) Irony
D) Plot twist

Answer: D) Plot twist

Explanation: A plot twist is a narrative device that introduces a sudden and unexpected change in the direction or outcome of the story, often surprising the audience or reader.

Question 82:

What is the chemical symbol for silver?

A) Ag

B) Si

C) Sr

D) Sn

Answer: A) Ag

Explanation: The chemical symbol for silver is Ag, derived from the Latin word "argentum."

Question 83:

Who wrote the novel "The Picture of Dorian Gray"?

A) Oscar Wilde

B) Virginia Woolf

C) James Joyce

D) D.H. Lawrence

Answer: A) Oscar Wilde

Explanation: "The Picture of Dorian Gray" is a novel written by Oscar Wilde, exploring themes of vanity, morality, and the pursuit of eternal youth.

Question 84:

What is the capital of Russia?

A) Moscow

B) Saint Petersburg

C) Novosibirsk

D) Yekaterinburg

Answer: A) Moscow

Explanation: Moscow is the capital city of Russia, known for its historic landmarks, iconic architecture, and cultural heritage.

Question 85:
What is the chemical symbol for calcium?
A) Ca
B) Cl
C) Cu
D) Cm

Answer: A) Ca

Explanation: The chemical symbol for calcium is Ca, derived from the Latin word "calx."

Question 86:
Who wrote the novel "The Hobbit"?
A) J.R.R. Tolkien
B) C.S. Lewis
C) J.K. Rowling
D) George R.R. Martin

Answer: A) J.R.R. Tolkien

Explanation: "The Hobbit" is a fantasy novel written by J.R.R. Tolkien, serving as a prequel to his epic high-fantasy series "The Lord of the Rings."

Question 87:
Which of the following terms refers to a word that is the opposite in meaning to another word?
A) Antonym
B) Synonym
C) Homonym
D) Homophone

Answer: A) Antonym

Explanation: An antonym is a word that has the opposite meaning of another word. For example, "hot" is an antonym of "cold."

Question 88:
What is the chemical symbol for nitrogen?
A) N
B) Ni
C) Na
D) Ne

Answer: A) N

Explanation: The chemical symbol for nitrogen is N, derived from the Greek word "nitron."

Question 89:
Who composed the famous piano piece "Für Elise"?
A) Ludwig van Beethoven
B) Wolfgang Amadeus Mozart
C) Frédéric Chopin
D) Johann Sebastian Bach

Answer: A) Ludwig van Beethoven

Explanation: "Für Elise" is a famous piano piece composed by Ludwig van Beethoven, known for its melodic simplicity and enduring popularity.

Question 90:
What is the plural form of "moose"?
A) Mooses
B) Meece
C) Meese
D) Moose

Answer: D) Moose

Explanation: The plural form of "moose" is also "moose," remaining the same in both singular and plural usage.

Question 91:
Who wrote the novel "Wuthering Heights"?
A) Emily Brontë
B) Charlotte Brontë
C) Anne Brontë
D) Jane Austen

Answer: A) Emily Brontë

Explanation: "Wuthering Heights" is a novel written by Emily Brontë, exploring themes of love, revenge, and the supernatural on the Yorkshire moors.

Question 92:
What is the chemical symbol for hydrogen?
A) H
B) Hy
C) He
D) Ho

Answer: A) H

Explanation: The chemical symbol for hydrogen is H, derived from the Greek word "hydrogenes."

Question 93:
Which of the following is an example of a primary color in the subtractive color model?
A) Cyan
B) Green
C) Yellow
D) Magenta

Answer: C) Yellow

Explanation: In the subtractive color model used in printing, the primary colors are cyan, magenta, and yellow.

Question 94:
Who is the author of "The Canterbury Tales"?
A) Geoffrey Chaucer
B) William Langland
C) John Gower
D) Thomas Malory

Answer: A) Geoffrey Chaucer

Explanation: "The Canterbury Tales" is a collection of stories written by Geoffrey Chaucer, providing insight into medieval English society.

Question 95:
What is the capital of India?
A) Delhi
B) Mumbai
C) Kolkata
D) Chennai

Answer: A) Delhi

Explanation: Delhi is the capital city of India, serving as the political, cultural, and historical center of the country.

Question 96:
Which of the following terms refers to a word that has the same or nearly the same meaning as another word?
A) Synonym
B) Antonym
C) Homonym
D) Homophone

Answer: A) Synonym

Explanation: A synonym is a word that has the same or nearly the same meaning as another word. For example, "happy" and "joyful" are synonyms.

Question 97:
What is the chemical symbol for carbon dioxide?
A) CO
B) CO2
C) O2
D) C2O

Answer: B) CO2

Explanation: The chemical formula for carbon dioxide is CO2, indicating one carbon atom bonded to two oxygen atoms.

Question 98:
Who wrote the novel "Brave New World"?
A) Aldous Huxley
B) George Orwell
C) Ray Bradbury
D) H.G. Wells

Answer: A) Aldous Huxley

Explanation: "Brave New World" is a dystopian novel written by Aldous Huxley, exploring themes of technological control, social conditioning, and individual freedom.

Question 99:
What is the plural form of "octopus"?
A) Octopuses
B) Octopi
C) Octopodes
D) Octopussies

Answer: A) Octopuses

Explanation: The plural form of "octopus" is "octopuses," following standard English pluralization rules.

Question 100:
Which of the following terms refers to the repetition of initial consonant sounds in nearby words?
A) Alliteration
B) Assonance
C) Consonance
D) Onomatopoeia

Answer: A) Alliteration

Explanation: Alliteration is a literary device that involves the repetition of initial consonant sounds in nearby words, creating a rhythmic or melodic effect.

Question 101:
What is the chemical symbol for potassium?
A) P
B) K
C) Po
D) Pt

Answer: B) K

Explanation: The chemical symbol for potassium is K, derived from the Latin word "kalium."

Question 102:
Who composed the famous opera "The Magic Flute"?
A) Wolfgang Amadeus Mozart
B) Ludwig van Beethoven
C) Richard Wagner
D) Giuseppe Verdi

Answer: A) Wolfgang Amadeus Mozart

Explanation: "The Magic Flute" is an opera composed by Wolfgang Amadeus Mozart, known for its enchanting music and fantastical storyline.

Question 103:
What is the capital of Australia?
A) Sydney
B) Melbourne
C) Canberra
D) Brisbane

Answer: C) Canberra

Explanation: Canberra is the capital city of Australia, located in the Australian Capital Territory.

Question 104:
Who wrote the novel "The Scarlet Letter"?
A) Nathaniel Hawthorne
B) Herman Melville
C) Emily Dickinson
D) Edgar Allan Poe

Answer: A) Nathaniel Hawthorne

Explanation: "The Scarlet Letter" is a novel written by Nathaniel Hawthorne, set in colonial Massachusetts and exploring themes of sin, guilt, and redemption.

Question 105:
What is the chemical symbol for gold?
A) Au
B) Ag
C) Fe
D) Pb

Answer: A) Au

Explanation: The chemical symbol for gold is Au, derived from the Latin word "aurum."

Question 106:
Which of the following is not a type of rock?
A) Igneous
B) Metamorphic
C) Fossiliferous
D) Sedimentary

Answer: C) Fossiliferous

Explanation: "Fossiliferous" refers to rocks containing fossils but is not a distinct category of rock like igneous, metamorphic, or sedimentary.

Question 107:
What is the plural form of "datum"?
A) Data
B) Datas
C) Datums
D) Datum's

Answer: A) Data

Explanation: The plural form of "datum" is "data," commonly used in both singular and plural contexts in modern English.

Question 108:
Who wrote the play "Othello"?
A) William Shakespeare
B) Christopher Marlowe
C) Ben Jonson
D) John Webster

Answer: A) William Shakespeare

Explanation: "Othello" is a tragedy written by William Shakespeare, depicting the tragic downfall of the noble Moorish general Othello.

Question 109:
What is the chemical symbol for tin?
A) Ti
B) T
C) Sn
D) Si

Answer: C) Sn

Explanation: The chemical symbol for tin is Sn, derived from the Latin word "stannum."

Question 110:
Which of the following terms refers to the arrangement of events or the structure of a story?
A) Plot
B) Theme
C) Tone
D) Characterization

Answer: A) Plot

Explanation: The plot of a story refers to the sequence of events and the arrangement of those events to create a narrative structure.

Question 111:
What is the chemical symbol for silver?
A) Ag
B) Au
C) Si
D) Sn

Answer: A) Ag

Explanation: The chemical symbol for silver is Ag, derived from the Latin word "argentum."

Question 112:

Who wrote the novel "To Kill a Mockingbird"?

A) Harper Lee

B) John Steinbeck

C) Ernest Hemingway

D) Truman Capote

Answer: A) Harper Lee

Explanation: "To Kill a Mockingbird" is a novel written by Harper Lee, exploring themes of racial injustice and moral growth in the American South.

Question 113:

What is the capital of Argentina?

A) Buenos Aires

B) Santiago

C) Montevideo

D) Lima

Answer: A) Buenos Aires

Explanation: Buenos Aires is the capital city of Argentina, known for its vibrant culture, historic architecture, and tango music.

Question 114:

Which of the following terms refers to the comparison of two unlike things using "like" or "as"?

A) Simile

B) Metaphor

C) Personification

D) Hyperbole

Answer: A) Simile

Explanation: A simile is a figure of speech that compares two unlike things using "like" or "as," such as "as brave as a lion."

Question 115:
What is the chemical symbol for potassium?
A) P
B) K
C) Po
D) Pt

Answer: B) K

Explanation: The chemical symbol for potassium is K, derived from the Latin word "kalium."

Question 116:
Who composed the famous ballet "The Nutcracker"?
A) Pyotr Ilyich Tchaikovsky
B) Ludwig van Beethoven
C) Igor Stravinsky
D) Sergei Prokofiev

Answer: A) Pyotr Ilyich Tchaikovsky

Explanation: "The Nutcracker" is a ballet composed by Pyotr Ilyich Tchaikovsky, featuring a magical Christmas-themed storyline.

Question 117:
What is the capital of Germany?
A) Berlin
B) Munich
C) Hamburg
D) Frankfurt

Answer: A) Berlin

Explanation: Berlin is the capital city of Germany, known for its rich history, cultural diversity, and vibrant arts scene.

Question 118:
Who wrote the play "The Importance of Being Earnest"?
A) Oscar Wilde
B) George Bernard Shaw
C) Samuel Beckett
D) Tom Stoppard

Answer: A) Oscar Wilde

Explanation: "The Importance of Being Earnest" is a comedic play written by Oscar Wilde, satirizing Victorian society and its social conventions.

Question 119:
What is the chemical symbol for iron?
A) Ir
B) Fe
C) In
D) Io

Answer: B) Fe

Explanation: The chemical symbol for iron is Fe, derived from the Latin word "ferrum."

Question 120:
What is the plural form of "child"?
A) Childs
B) Children
C) Childes
D) Child's

Answer: B) Children

Explanation: The plural form of "child" is "children," following irregular pluralization rules.

Question 121:
Which of the following terms refers to a long narrative poem, typically about heroic deeds or events of great significance?
A) Epic
B) Sonnet
C) Haiku
D) Limerick

Answer: A) Epic

Explanation: An epic is a long narrative poem that celebrates heroic deeds, legendary figures, or significant events in a grand and elevated style.

Question 122:
Who is the author of the novel "Pride and Prejudice"?
A) Jane Austen
B) Charlotte Brontë
C) Emily Brontë
D) Elizabeth Gaskell

Answer: A) Jane Austen

Explanation: "Pride and Prejudice" is a novel written by Jane Austen, exploring themes of love, class, and societal expectations in Regency-era England.

Question 123:
What is the chemical symbol for helium?
A) He
B) H
C) Ha
D) Hy

Answer: A) He

Explanation: The chemical symbol for helium is He, derived from the Greek word "helios."

Question 124:
Who composed the famous symphony "Symphony No. 5"?
A) Ludwig van Beethoven
B) Wolfgang Amadeus Mozart
C) Johann Sebastian Bach
D) Franz Schubert

Answer: A) Ludwig van Beethoven

Explanation: "Symphony No. 5" is a symphony composed by Ludwig van Beethoven, featuring the iconic four-note motif in the opening movement.

Question 125:
What is the plural form of "deer"?
A) Deers
B) Deer
C) Dears
D) Dear

Answer: B) Deer

Explanation: The plural form of "deer" remains the same as the singular, following irregular pluralization rules.

Question 126:
Who wrote the play "Hamlet"?
A) William Shakespeare
B) Christopher Marlowe
C) Ben Jonson
D) John Donne

Answer: A) William Shakespeare

Explanation: "Hamlet" is a tragedy written by William Shakespeare, featuring Prince Hamlet's quest for revenge against his uncle, Claudius.

Question 127:
What is the chemical symbol for sulfur?
A) Su
B) Sf
C) S
D) Sl

Answer: C) S

Explanation: The chemical symbol for sulfur is S, derived from the Latin word "sulfurium."

Question 128:
Which of the following terms refers to a story that explains the origins of natural phenomena, beliefs, or customs?
A) Myth
B) Legend
C) Fable
D) Folktale

Answer: A) Myth

Explanation: A myth is a traditional story that explains the origins of natural phenomena, beliefs, or customs, often involving gods, heroes, and supernatural beings.

Question 129:
What is the capital of Brazil?
A) Rio de Janeiro
B) São Paulo
C) Brasília
D) Salvador

Answer: C) Brasília

Explanation: Brasília is the capital city of Brazil, known for its modernist architecture and urban planning.

Question 130:
Who wrote the novel "The Catcher in the Rye"?
A) J.D. Salinger
B) F. Scott Fitzgerald
C) Ernest Hemingway
D) John Steinbeck

Answer: A) J.D. Salinger

Explanation: "The Catcher in the Rye" is a novel written by J.D. Salinger, featuring the protagonist Holden Caulfield's journey through adolescence and alienation.

Question 131:
What is the chemical symbol for phosphorus?
A) Ph
B) Po
C) Ps
D) P

Answer: D) P

Explanation: The chemical symbol for phosphorus is P, derived from the Greek word "phosphoros."

Question 132:
Who composed the famous symphony "Symphony No. 9"?
A) Ludwig van Beethoven
B) Wolfgang Amadeus Mozart
C) Franz Schubert
D) Johannes Brahms

Answer: A) Ludwig van Beethoven

Explanation: "Symphony No. 9," also known as the "Choral Symphony," is a symphony composed by Ludwig van Beethoven, featuring the "Ode to Joy" in its final movement.

Question 133:
What is the capital of Italy?
A) Rome
B) Milan
C) Florence
D) Venice

Answer: A) Rome

Explanation: Rome is the capital city of Italy, known for its rich history, ancient ruins, and iconic landmarks such as the Colosseum and Vatican City.

Question 134:
Who wrote the novel "Moby-Dick"?
A) Herman Melville
B) Nathaniel Hawthorne
C) Edgar Allan Poe
D) Emily Dickinson

Answer: A) Herman Melville

Explanation: "Moby-Dick" is a novel written by Herman Melville, exploring themes of obsession, fate, and the human condition through the character Captain Ahab's pursuit of the white whale.

Question 135:
What is the chemical symbol for aluminum?
A) Al
B) Au
C) Ag
D) Am

Answer: A) Al

Explanation: The chemical symbol for aluminum is Al, derived from the Latin word "alumen."

Question 136:
Which of the following terms refers to the use of vivid or figurative language to represent objects, actions, or ideas?
A) Imagery
B) Symbolism
C) Allegory
D) Allusion

Answer: A) Imagery

Explanation: Imagery refers to the use of vivid or figurative language to represent objects, actions, or ideas, appealing to the senses to create a mental picture for the reader.

Question 137:
What is the chemical symbol for copper?
A) Co
B) Cu
C) Cp
D) Cr

Answer: B) Cu

Explanation: The chemical symbol for copper is Cu, derived from the Latin word "cuprum."

Question 138:
Who composed the famous opera "Carmen"?
A) Georges Bizet
B) Giuseppe Verdi
C) Wolfgang Amadeus Mozart
D) Richard Wagner

Answer: A) Georges Bizet

Explanation: "Carmen" is an opera composed by Georges Bizet, featuring the tragic love story of the fiery gypsy Carmen and the soldier Don José.

Question 139:

What is the capital of Egypt?

A) Cairo

B) Alexandria

C) Luxor

D) Giza

Answer: A) Cairo

Explanation: Cairo is the capital city of Egypt, known for its historic landmarks such as the Great Pyramids of Giza and the Sphinx.

Question 140:

Who wrote the novel "The Grapes of Wrath"?

A) John Steinbeck

B) Ernest Hemingway

C) F. Scott Fitzgerald

D) William Faulkner

Answer: A) John Steinbeck

Explanation: "The Grapes of Wrath" is a novel written by John Steinbeck, depicting the struggles of the Joad family during the Great Depression.

Question 141:

What is the chemical symbol for zinc?

A) Zc

B) Zn

C) Zi

D) Zm

Answer: B) Zn

Explanation: The chemical symbol for zinc is Zn, derived from the German word "zink."

Question 142:
Which of the following terms refers to the use of words that imitate sounds associated with the objects or actions they refer to?
A) Onomatopoeia
B) Alliteration
C) Metaphor
D) Simile

Answer: A) Onomatopoeia

Explanation: Onomatopoeia is a literary device that involves the use of words that imitate sounds associated with the objects or actions they refer to, such as "buzz" or "bang."

Question 143:
What is the capital of South Korea?
A) Seoul
B) Busan
C) Incheon
D) Daegu

Answer: A) Seoul

Explanation: Seoul is the capital city of South Korea, known for its modern architecture, vibrant culture, and historical landmarks.

Question 144:
Who wrote the novel "1984"?
A) George Orwell
B) Aldous Huxley
C) Ray Bradbury
D) Margaret Atwood

Answer: A) George Orwell

Explanation: "1984" is a dystopian novel written by George Orwell, depicting a totalitarian regime and exploring themes of surveillance, censorship, and governmental control.

Question 145:
What is the chemical symbol for mercury?
A) Me
B) Mg
C) Hg
D) Mn

Answer: C) Hg

Explanation: The chemical symbol for mercury is Hg, derived from the Greek word "hydrargyrum."

Question 146:
Which of the following terms refers to a brief and indirect reference to a person, place, thing, or idea of historical, cultural, literary, or political significance?
A) Allusion
B) Allegory
C) Metaphor
D) Simile

Answer: A) Allusion

Explanation: An allusion is a brief and indirect reference to a person, place, thing, or idea of historical, cultural, literary, or political significance, often enriching the meaning of the text.

Question 147:
What is the chemical symbol for sodium?
A) Sa
B) So
C) Sd
D) Na

Answer: D) Na

Explanation: The chemical symbol for sodium is Na, derived from the Latin word "natrium."

Question 148:
Who composed the famous ballet "Swan Lake"?
A) Pyotr Ilyich Tchaikovsky
B) Igor Stravinsky
C) Sergei Prokofiev
D) Claude Debussy

Answer: A) Pyotr Ilyich Tchaikovsky

Explanation: "Swan Lake" is a ballet composed by Pyotr Ilyich Tchaikovsky, featuring a tragic love story between Prince Siegfried and Odette, the Swan Queen.

Question 149:
What is the capital of Spain?
A) Madrid
B) Barcelona
C) Seville
D) Valencia

Answer: A) Madrid

Explanation: Madrid is the capital city of Spain, known for its rich cultural heritage, art museums, and vibrant nightlife.

Question 150:
Who wrote the novel "The Great Gatsby"?
A) F. Scott Fitzgerald
B) Ernest Hemingway
C) John Steinbeck
D) William Faulkner

Answer: A) F. Scott Fitzgerald

Explanation: "The Great Gatsby" is a novel written by F. Scott Fitzgerald, depicting the Jazz Age in America and exploring themes of love, wealth, and the American Dream.

.

Made in United States
Orlando, FL
02 October 2024